C++

A Detailed Approach to Practical Coding

Nathan Clark

© Copyright 2017 by Nathan Clark
- All rights reserved.

This document is presented with the desire to provide reliable, quality information about the topic in question and the facts discussed within. This book is sold under the assumption that neither the author nor the publisher should be asked to provide the services discussed within. If any discussion, professional or legal, is otherwise required a proper professional should be consulted.

This Declaration was held acceptable and equally approved by the Committee of Publishers and Associations as well as the American Bar Association.

The reproduction, duplication or transmission of any of the included information is considered illegal whether done in print or electronically. Creating a recorded copy or a secondary copy of this work is also prohibited unless the action of doing so is first cleared through the Publisher and condoned in writing. All rights reserved.

Any information contained in the following pages is considered accurate and truthful and that any liability through inattention or by any use or misuse of the topics discussed within falls solely on the reader. There are no cases in which the Publisher of this work can be held responsible or be asked to provide reparations for any loss of monetary gain or other damages which may be caused by following the presented information in any way shape or form.

The following information is presented purely for informative purposes and is therefore considered universal. The information presented within is done so without a contract or any other type of assurance as to its quality or validity.

Any trademarks which are used are done so without consent and any use of the same does not imply consent or permission was gained from the owner. Any trademarks or brands found within are purely used for clarification purposes and no owners are in anyway affiliated with this work.

Books in this Series

C++: Programming Basics for Absolute Beginners

C++: A Detailed Approach to Practical Coding

Table of Contents

Introduction --- 1
1. Data Types -- 3
2. Variable Scope --- 13
3. Constants and Literals --------------------------------------- 17
4. Signed and Unsigned Data Types ------------------------------ 27
5. Operators --- 31
6. Numbers -- 45
7. Strings -- 59
8. Functions --- 83
9. Classes and Objects --------------------------------------- 89
10. Arrays -- 115
11. Data Structure --- 127
12. Pointers --- 133
13. Date and Time -- 139
Conclusion -- 143

Introduction

This book is the second book in the Step-By-Step C++ series. If you haven't read the first book *C++: Programming Basics for Absolute Beginners*, I highly suggest you do so before getting into this book.

In this intermediate level guide we will delve more into further concepts of C++. With each topic we will look at a detailed description, proper syntax and numerous examples to make your learning experience as easy as possible. C++ is a wonderful programming language and I trust you will enjoy this book as much as I enjoyed writing it. So without further ado, let's get started!

1. Data Types

Data types are used in programming languages to store different types of data. For example if you wanted to store text data, then you would probably have a data type of 'string'. If you wanted to store a number you can have a data type of say 'number' or 'integer'. This depends on the programming language and what are the data types they define. Data types help to make the program type safe and free from errors.

Now let's look at the different data types available in C++.

Table 1: Data types

Keyword	Description
bool	This is used to define a value which can have the value of 1(true) or 0(false).
char	This is used to define a value which can have a character value such as 'A' or 'a'.
Int	This is used to define a value which can have a number value such as 1.
float	This is used to define a value which can have a decimal value such as 12.53.

Keyword	Description
double	This is used to define a value which can have a larger decimal value such as 3.141592653589793.

Now let's look at an example of how we can use data types in C++ programs.

Example 1: The following program is used to showcase the definition of the various data types in C++.

```
#include <iostream>

int main() {

// This line defines a variable of the boolean data type
    bool status=true;

// This line defines a variable of the character data type

    char c='A';

// This line defines a variable of the Integer data type

    int i=1;

// This line defines a variable of the float data type

    float f=12.34;

// This line defines a variable of the double data type

    double d=12.3333;
```

```
//We now send each value to the standard output

    std::cout << "This is a boolean value " << status << std::endl;

    std::cout << "This is a charater value " << c << std::endl;

    std::cout << "This is a integer value " << i << std::endl;

    std::cout << "This is a float value " << f << std::endl;

    std::cout << "This is a double value " << d << std::endl;

    return 0;

}
```

With this program, the output is as follows:

This is a boolean value 1
This is a charater value A
This is a integer value 1
This is a float value 12.34
This is a double value 12.3333

1.1 Size of a data type and signed / unsigned data types

Each data type has a size allocated to it which is used to store the value associated with the data type. This size is fixed for each data type.

The below table gives an example of the width of each data type.

Table 2: Data types size

Type	Width
char	1 byte
unsigned char	1 byte
int	4bytes
unsigned int	4bytes
signed int	4bytes
float	4bytes
double	8bytes

Now let's see how we can write a C++ program that can be used to get the size of variables which are defined of a particular data type.

Example 2: The following program is used to showcase the way we can get the size of each data type.

```
#include <iostream>

int main() {

    bool status=true;

    char c='A';
```

```
    int i=1;

    float f=12.34;

    double d=12.3333;


    std::cout << "The size of the boolean value is " << sizeof(status) << std::endl;

    std::cout << "The size of the charater value is " << sizeof(c) << std::endl;

    std::cout << "The size of the integer value is " << sizeof(i) << std::endl;

    std::cout << "The size of the float value is " << sizeof(f) << std::endl;

    std::cout << "The size of the double value is " << sizeof(d) << std::endl;

    return 0;
}
```

The sizeof function is an inbuilt C++ function that can be used to get the size in bytes of a variable.

With this program, the output is as follows:

The size of the boolean value is 1
The size of the charater value is 1
The size of the integer value is 4
The size of the float value is 4
The size of the double value is 8

1.2 Data types ranges

Each data type, based on the number of bytes, also has a limitation on the range of values that can be defined. The below table gives the range of possible values for each defined data type in C++.

Table 3: Data types ranges

Type	Range
char	-128 to 127 or 0 to 255
int	-2147483648 to 2147483647
float	+/- 3.4e +/- 38
double	+/- 1.7e +/- 308

Example 3: The following program is used to showcase the ranges for the different data types.

```
#include <iostream>

int main() {

   char c1=244;
   int i1=2147483647;
   float f1=3.4e+30;
   double d1=3.4e+300;

std::cout << "The character value is " << int(c1) << std::endl;

std::cout << "The integer value is " << i1 << std::endl;
std::cout << "The float value is " << f1 << std::endl;
std::cout << "The double value is " << d1 << std::endl;
```

```
    return 0;
}
```

With this program, the output is as follows:

The character value is -12

The integer value is 2147483647

The float value is 3.4e+030

The double value is 3.4e+300

1.3 Enum data type

The enum data type is used to define a custom data type. When you want to define custom values, then one can define an enum type. In the example below, there is a requirement to define a type which can store the days of the week.

Since the days of the week cannot be stored in the data types we have already seen, we need to define this using the enum type.

Example 4: The following program is used to showcase the way to use enum types.

```
#include <iostream>

int main() {
  enum Daysoftheweek
  {
    Sunday, // assigned a value of 0
    Monday, // assigned a value of 1
    Tuesday, // assigned a value of 2
```

```
    Wednesday, // assigned a value of 3
    Thursday, // assigned a value of 4
    Friday, // assigned a value of 5
    Saturday // assigned a value of 6
}; // The enum has to end with a semi colon

Daysoftheweek holiday = Sunday;

std::cout << " The holiday day of the week is " << holiday << std::endl;

return 0;
}
```

Some of the key aspects which need to be noted about the above program:

- All the values for the enum type collection are defined in the curly braces.

- Internally the first value of the collection will be assigned an integer value of 0.

- The enum type needs to end with a semi colon.

- One can define variables of the enum type.

With this program, the output is as follows:

The holiday day of the week is 0

Now let's look at another example of the enum type. But this time we are going to explicitly define the value for the first item in the enum collection.

Example 5: The following program is used to define the starting value of the first item in the enum collection.

```
#include <iostream>

int main() {
   enum Daysoftheweek
   {
      Sunday=-3, // assigned a value of -3
      Monday, // assigned a value of -2
      Tuesday, // assigned a value of -1
      Wednesday, // assigned a value of 0
      Thursday, // assigned a value of 1
      Friday, // assigned a value of 2
      Saturday // assigned a value of 3
   }; // The enum has to end with a semi colon

   Daysoftheweek holiday = Friday;

   std::cout << " The holiday day of the week is " << holiday << std::endl;

   return 0;
}
```

In the above program one can see that we are explicitly defining the value of the first item in the collection to value of -3. The rest of the items in the collection will get the subsequent integer values.

With this program, the output is as follows:

The holiday day of the week is 2

Now let's look at another example wherein we can loop through the values of the enum type if we don't want to show the integer value but the actual item in the enum collection.

Example 6: The following program is used to use conditions to see the value corresponding to the item in the enum collection.

```
#include <iostream>

int main() {
  enum Daysoftheweek
  {
    Sunday,
    Monday,
    Tuesday,
    Wednesday,
    Thursday,
    Friday,
    Saturday
  };

  Daysoftheweek holiday;

  if (holiday == Sunday) std::cout << "Sunday";
  else if (holiday == Monday) std::cout << "Monday";
  else if (holiday == Tuesday) std::cout << "Tuesday";
  else if (holiday == Wednesday) std::cout << "Wednesday";
  else if (holiday == Thursday) std::cout << "Thursday";
  else if (holiday == Friday) std::cout << "Friday";
  else std::cout << "Saturday";
  return 0;
}
```

2. Variable Scope

Variables in a c++ program have a scope. They can either have a local or a global scope. When a variable has a global scope they can be defined anywhere in the program. Whereas if the variable has a local scope then they can only be used in the block of code in which they are defined.

Let's now look at an example of local and global variables.

Example 7: The following program is used to show local and global variables.

```
#include <iostream>

int main() {

    int gvalue=10;

    {

    int lvalue=20;

    std::cout << "The value of the local variable is " << lvalue << std::endl;

    }

    std::cout << "The value of the global variable is " << gvalue <<
```

```
    std::endl;

    return 0;
}
```

Now since the variable lvalue is defined after the second curly braces, it is only available to the block of code before the next ending curly braces.

With this program, the output is as follows:

The value of the local variable is 20
The value of the global variable is 10

Let's now look at the same example and try to make an error in the program to confirm our understanding on local and global variables.

Example 8: The following program is used to show local and global variables define wrongly.

```
#include <iostream>

int main() {

    int gvalue=10;

    {

    int lvalue=20;

    std::cout << "The value of the local variable is " << lvalue << std::endl;

    }
```

```
    std::cout << "The value of the global variable is " << gvalue <<
std::endl;

    std::cout << "The value of the local variable is " << lvalue <<
std::endl;


    return 0;
}
```

With this program, the output is as follows:

In function 'int main()':

error: 'lvalue' was not declared in this scope

std::cout << "The value of the local variable is " <<
lvalue << std::endl;

As rightly so, there is an error in the program because we are trying to use the lvalue outside of the module in which it is defined.

3. Constants and Literals

A constant is referred to a value that cannot be changed. The literal is the most common type of constant. These are used to specify a type of literal. There are different types of literals which are classified below.

An integer literal can be a decimal, octal, or hexadecimal constant. An integer literal can also have a suffix that is a combination of U and L, for unsigned and long, respectively.

Example 9: The following program is used to showcase the way we can define constants.

```
#include <iostream>

int main() {

    //This is used to define a floating constant value

    const float f=3.14;

    //This is used to define an integer constant value

    const int i=3;

    std::cout << "The value of the floating constant is " << f << std::endl;

    std::cout << "The value of the integer constant is " << i <<
```

```
    std::endl;

    f=4.145;

    i=4;

    return 0;
}
```

With this program, the output is as follows:

The value of the floating constant is 3.14
The value of the integer constant is 3

Now let's look at another example which can confirm our understanding of constants.

Example 10: The following program is used to showcase an error condition when using constants.

```
#include <iostream>

int main() {

    //This is used to define a floating constant value

    const float f=3.14;

    //This is used to define an integer constant value

    const int i=3;

    std::cout << "The value of the floating constant is " << f << std::endl;
```

```
    std::cout << "The value of the integer constant is " << i << std::endl;

    f=4.145;

    i=4;

    return 0;
}
```

With this program, the output is as follows:

error: assignment of read-only variable 'f' f=4.145;

error: assignment of read-only variable 'i' i=4;

We rightly so get an error because we are trying to change the value of constants which cannot be changed as per their definition.

Now let's look at the use of literals. We have different types of literals and let's look at each one of them in more detail.

3.1 Integer literals

Example 11: The following program is used to showcase the use of integer literals.

```
#include <iostream>

int main() {

    //This is used to define an unsigned integer literal

    int i=100U;
```

```
//This is used to define a long integer literal

int i1=100L;

//This is used to define an unsigned long integer literal

int i2=100UL;

    std::cout << "The value of the unsigned integer literal is " << i << std::endl;

    std::cout << "The value of the long integer literal is " << i1 << std::endl;

    std::cout << "The value of the unsigned long integer literal is " << i2 << std::endl;

    return 0;

}
```

With this program, the output is as follows:

The value of the unsigned integer literal is 100
The value of the long integer literal is 100
The value of the unsigned long integer literal is 100

Example 12: The following program is used to showcase how to use hexadecimal and octal literals.

```
#include <iostream>

int main() {
```

```
    //This is used to define an octal literal

    int i=0313;

    //This is used to define a hexadecimal literal

    int i1=0x3c;

    std::cout << "The value of the octal literal is " << i << std::endl;

    std::cout << "The value of the hexadecimal literal is " << i1 << std::endl;

    return 0;
}
```

With this program, the output is as follows:

The value of the unsigned integer literal is 203

The value of the long integer literal is 60

3.2 Floating point literals

A floating-point literal has an integer part, a decimal point, a fractional part, and an exponent part. The floating point literals can be represented either in decimal form or exponential form.

Example 13: The following program is used to showcase the use of floating point literals.

```
#include <iostream>

int main() {

    //This is used to define a floating point literal with a decimal point

    float f=3.14;

    //This is used to define a floating point literal with an exponential point

    float f2=314567E2;

    std::cout << "The value of the floating point literal with a decimal point is " << f << std::endl;

    std::cout << "The value of the floating point literal with an exponential point is " << f2 << std::endl;

    return 0;

}
```

With this program, the output is as follows:

The value of the floating point literal with a decimal point is 3.14

The value of the floating point literal with an exponential point is 3.14567e+007

3.3 Character literals

A character literal is enclosed within single quotes. Also in addition to defining normal characters you can also define escape sequences. So for example, if you wanted to have a new line character, you would define the character as /n.

Below is the table for the various escape sequences.

Table 4: Escape sequences

Escape sequence	Meaning
\\	This defines the \ character
\'	This defines the ' character
\"	This defines the " character
\?	This defines the ? character
\a	This defines the alert or bell
\b	This defines the backspace character
\f	This defines the form feed character
\n	This defines the new line character
\r	This defines the carriage return character
\t	This defines the horizontal tab
\v	This defines the vertical tab

Example 14: The following program is used to showcase character literals.

```
#include <iostream>

int main() {

    //This is used to define a character literal

    char c='B';

    std::cout << "The value of the floating constant is " << c << std::endl;

    std::cout << "An example of the tab and new line escape sequence\tis\nshown below";

    return 0;

}
```

With this program, the output is as follows:

The value of the floating constant is B
An example of the tab and new line escape sequence is
shown below

3.4 String literals
String literals are nothing but a series of characters.

Example 15: *The following program is used to showcase string literals.*

```
#include <iostream>

int main() {

    std::cout << "An example of a string literal \tis\nshown below";

    return 0;
}
```

With this program, the output is as follows:

An example of a string literal is

shown below

4. Signed and Unsigned Data Types

For some of the data types, such as the char and integer you have a further classification:

- One is the breaking of an integer into a short and long integer.

- And next is the ability to add signs for a value to indicate whether it is a signed or unsigned value.

Table 5: Data types ranges for short, long, signed and unsigned

Type	Range
char	-128 to 127 or 0 to 255
unsigned char	0 to 255
signed char	-128 to 127
int	-2147483648 to 2147483647
unsigned int	0 to 4294967295

Type	Range
signed int	-2147483648 to 2147483647
short int	-32768 to 32767
unsigned short int	0 to 65,535
signed short int	-32768 to 32767
long int	-9,223,372,036,854,775,808 to 9,223,372,036,854,775,807
signed long int	-9,223,372,036,854,775,808 to 9,223,372,036,854,775,807
unsigned long int	0 to 18,446,744,073,709,551,615
float	+/- 3.4e +/- 38
double	+/- 1.7e +/- 308

Example 16: The following program is used to showcase the way we can define unsigned and signed values in C++.

```
#include <iostream>

int main() {

    unsigned char c1=244;

    signed char c2=-100;

    unsigned int i1=1;

    signed int i2=-11;
```

```
std::cout << "An example of an unsigned character value is " << int(c1) << std::endl;

std::cout << "An example of a signed character value is " << int(c2) << std::endl;
std::cout << "An example of an unsigned integer value is " << i1 << std::endl;
std::cout << "An example of a signed integer value is " << i2 << std::endl;

   return 0;

}
```

With this program, the output is as follows:

An example of an unsigned character value is 244

An example of a signed character value is -100

An example of an unsigned integer value is 1

An example of a signed integer value is -11

Example 17: The following program is used to showcase the way we can use short and long integers in a C++ program.

```
#include <iostream>

int main() {

   short int i1=1;

   long int i2=110000000;
```

```
    std::cout << "An example of a short integer value is " << int(i1)
<< std::endl;

    std::cout << "An example of a long integer value is " << int(i2) <<
std::endl;

    return 0;

}
```

5. Operators

There are various types of operators available in C++. The operators help in carrying out various operations on the defined variables in a C++ program. Let's look at each of the operators in more detail.

5.1 Arithmetic operators

These are operators that are used to work with numbers. The most common operators are shown below.

Table 6: Arithmetic operators

Operator	Operation
+	This is used to add two operands
-	This is used to subtract one operand from another
*	This is used to multiple two operands
/	This is used to divide one operand by another
%	This gives the remainder value after a division operator

Operator	Operation
++	This is used to increment a value by one
--	This is used to decrement a value by one

Example 18: The following program is used to showcase the way we can use arithmetic operators.

```
#include <iostream>

int main() {

   // Defining 2 operands
   int i=10;

   int j=3;

   std::cout << "The addition of the two operands is  " << i+j << std::endl;

   std::cout << "The subtraction of the two operands is  " << i-j << std::endl;

   std::cout << "The multiplication of the two operands is  " << i*j << std::endl;

   std::cout << "The division of the two operands is  " << i/j << std::endl;

   std::cout << "The remainder after division of the two operands is " << i%j << std::endl;

   std::cout << "Incrementing operand one by one  " << i++ << std::endl;
```

```
    std::cout << "Decrementing operand two by one " << j-- <<
std::endl;

    return 0;

}
```

With this program, the output is as follows:

The addition of the two operands is 13

The subtraction of the two operands is 7

The multiplication of the two operands is 30

The division of the two operands is 3

The remainder after division of the two operands is 1

Incrementing operand one by one 10

Decrementing operand two by one 3

5.2 Relational operators

These are operators that are used to determine the value of conditions based on the value of the operands. The relational operators possible in C++ are given below.

Table 7: Relational operators

Operator	Operation
==	This is used to check if two operands are equal

Operator	Operation
!=	This is used to check if two operands are not equal
>	This is used to check if one operand is greater than the other
<	This is used to check if one operand is less than the other
>=	This is used to check if one operand is greater than or equal to the other
<=	This is used to check if one operand is less than or equal to the other

If a condition evaluates to true, then a value of 1 is returned else a value of 0 is returned.

Example 19: The following program is used to showcase the way we can use relational operators.

```
#include <iostream>

int main() {

    // Defining 2 operands
    int i=10;

    int j=3;

    std::cout << "Is i equal to j = " << (i==j) << std::endl;

    std::cout << "Is i not equal to j = " << (i!=j) << std::endl;
```

```
    std::cout << "Is i greater than j = " << (i>j) << std::endl;

    std::cout << "Is i less than j = " << (i<j) << std::endl;

    std::cout << "Is i greater than or equal j = " << (i>=j) << std::endl;

    std::cout << "Is i less than or equal j = " << (i<=j) << std::endl;

    return 0;
}
```

With this program, the output is as follows:

Is i equal to j = 0
Is i not equal to j = 1
Is i greater than j = 1
Is i less than j = 0
Is i greater than or equal j = 1
Is i less than or equal j = 0

5.3 Logical operators

These are operators that are used to determine the value of conditions based on the value of the operands, where the operands are Boolean values. The logical operators possible in C++ are given below.

Table 8: Relational operators

Operator	Operation
&&	This is the logical AND operator
||	This is the logical OR operator
!	This is the Logical NOT operator

Below is the table for the logical operators based on the value of the operands for the AND operator.

Table 8.1: Relational operators - AND

Operand A	Operand B	Result
True	True	1
True	False	0
False	True	0
False	False	0

Example 20: The following program is used to showcase the way we can use logical operators for the AND operator.

```
#include <iostream>

int main() {

    // Defining 3 operands
    bool i=true;
```

```
    bool j=true;

    bool k=false;

// show casing the AND operator
    std::cout << "i AND j = " << (i && j) << std::endl;

    std::cout << "i AND k = " << (i && k) << std::endl;

    std::cout << "k AND i = " << (k && i) << std::endl;

    std::cout << "k AND k = " << (k && k) << std::endl;

    return 0;

}
```

With this program, the output is as follows:

i AND j = 1
i AND k = 0
k AND i = 0
k AND k = 0

Below is the table for the logical operators based on the value of the operands for the OR operator.

Table 8.2: Relational operators - OR

Operand A	Operand B	Result
True	True	1
True	False	1

Operand A	Operand B	Result
False	True	1
False	False	0

Example 21: The following program is used to showcase the way we can use logical operators for the OR operator.

```
#include <iostream>

int main() {

    // Defining 3 operands
    bool i=true;

    bool j=true;

    bool k=false;

// show casing the OR operator
    std::cout << "i OR j = " << (i && j) << std::endl;

    std::cout << "i OR k = " << (i && k) << std::endl;

    std::cout << "k OR i = " << (k && i) << std::endl;

    std::cout << "k OR k = " << (k && k) << std::endl;

    return 0;

}
```

With this program, the output is as follows:

i OR j = 1
i OR k = 0
k OR i = 0
k OR k = 0

Below is the table for the logical operators based on the value of the operands for the NOT operator.

Table 8.3: Relational operators - NOT

Operand A	Result
True	0
False	1

Example 22: The following program is used to showcase the way we can use logical operators for the NOT operator.

```
#include <iostream>

int main() {

  // Defining 2 operands
  bool i=true;

  bool j=false;

// show casing the NOT operator
  std::cout << " NOT i = " << (!i) << std::endl;

  std::cout << "NOT j = " << (!j) << std::endl;
```

```
    return 0;
}
```

With this program, the output is as follows:

NOT i = 0
NOT j = 1

5.4 Assignment operators

These are operators that are used to make assignment operations easier. The assignment operators possible in C++ are given below.

Table 9: Assignment operators

Operator	Operation
=	This is used to assign the value of an operation to an operand.
+=	This is used to carry out the addition and assignment operator in one go.
-=	This is used to carry out the subtraction and assignment operator in one go.
*=	This is used to carry out the multiplication and assignment operator in one go.
/=	This is used to carry out the division and assignment operator in one go.

Operator	Operation
%=	This is used to carry out the modulus and assignment operator in one go.

Now let's look at how we can implement these operators in further detail.

Example 23: The following program is used to showcase the way we can use assignment operators.

```
#include <iostream>

int main() {

    // Defining 3 operands
    int i=5;

    int j=10;

    int k;

// show casing the Assignment operators
    std::cout << "The value of i+j is " << (k=i+j) << std::endl;

    std::cout << "The value of i+=j is " << (i+=j) << std::endl;

    std::cout << "The value of i-=j is " << (i-=j) << std::endl;

    std::cout << "The value of i*=j is " << (i*=j) << std::endl;

    std::cout << "The value of i/=j is " << (i/=j) << std::endl;

    std::cout << "The value of i%=j is " << (i%=j) << std::endl;
```

```
    return 0;
}
```

With this program, the output is as follows:

The value of i+j is 15
The value of i+=j is 15
The value of i-=j is 5
The value of i*=j is 50
The value of i/=j is 5
The value of i%=j is 5

5.5 Bitwise operators

These are operators that are used to make bit operations on operands. The assignment operators possible in C++ are given below.

Table 10: Bitwise operators

Operator	Operation
&	This copies a bit to the result if it exists in both operands
|	This copies a bit to the result if it exists in either operands
^	This copies a bit to the result if it exists in one operands but not in both

Operator	Operation
<<	Here the left operands value is moved left by the number of bits specified by the right operand
>>	Here the left operands value is moved right by the number of bits specified by the right operand

Example 24: The following program is used to showcase the way we can use bitwise operators.

```
#include <iostream>

int main() {

  // Defining 3 operands
  int i=5;

  int j=10;

  int k;

// show casing the bitwise operators
  std::cout << "Showcasing the & bit operator " << (i & j) << std::endl;

  std::cout << "Showcasing the | bit operator " << (i | j) << std::endl;

  std::cout << "Showcasing the ^ bit operator " << (i ^ j) << std::endl;

  std::cout << "Showcasing the << bit operator " << (i<<2) <<
```

```
std::endl;

   std::cout << "Showcasing the >> bit operator " << (i>>2) << std::endl;

   return 0;

}
```

With this program, the output is as follows:

Showcasing the & bit operator 0
Showcasing the | bit operator 15
Showcasing the ^ bit operator 15
Showcasing the << bit operator 20
Showcasing the >> bit operator 1

6. Numbers

We have already looked at numbers in the data types chapter, but let's have a refresher on the different types of numbers available in C++.

Table 11: Bitwise operators

Data type	Description
short	This is used to define a short integer which has the range of -32768 to 32767
int	This is used to define an integer which has the range of -2147483648 to 2147483647
long	This is used to define a long integer which has the range of -9,223,372,036,854,775,808 to 9,223,372,036,854,775,807
float	This is used to define a floating point number which has the range of +/- 3.4e +/- 38
double	This is used to define a double point number which has the range of +/- 1.7e +/- 308

Example 25: The following program is used to showcase the basic way we can use these data types.

```cpp
#include <iostream>

int main() {

    // Defining variables of different data types
    short a=12;

    int  b=10000;

    long c=313444;

    float d=12.54;
    double e=12e12;


    std::cout << "Showcasing the short integer type " << a << std::endl;

    std::cout << "Showcasing the integer type " << b << std::endl;

    std::cout << "Showcasing the long integer type " << c << std::endl;

    std::cout << "Showcasing the floating type " << d << std::endl;

    std::cout << "Showcasing the double type " << e << std::endl;

    return 0;

}
```

With this program, the output is as follows:

Showcasing the short integer type 12

Showcasing the integer type 10000

Showcasing the long integer type 313444

Showcasing the floating type 12.54

Showcasing the double type 1.2e+013

6.1 Number functions

There are a number of built-in functions that can be used on numbers. Let's look at the vast majority of functions available for numbers.

6.1.1 Basic Functions

The below table gives the basic functions which are available for numbers.

Table 12: Basic functions

Function	Description
abs	This function is used to find the absolute value of a floating point number. This function will return an integer
fma	This function gives the fused multiply-add operation via the formula (x+y)*a
fmax	This function provides the larger of two floating point values

Function	Description
fmin	This function provides the smaller of two floating point values
fdim	This function provides the positive difference of two floating point values via the formula (max(0, x-y))

Example 26: The following program is used to showcase the way we can use basic function.

```
#include <iostream>
#include <cstdlib>
#include <cmath>

int main() {

  int a=2;
  int b=3;
  int c=4;
  float d=12.54;


  std::cout << "An example of fused multiply-add operation is " << fma(a,b,c) << std::endl;

  std::cout << "The larger of two floating point values is " << fmax(a,b) << std::endl;

  std::cout << "The minimum larger of two floating point values is " << fmin(a,b) << std::endl;

  std::cout << "The minimum difference of two floating point values is " << fdim(a,b) << std::endl;
```

```
    std::cout << "Absolute value " << abs(d) << std::endl;

    return 0;
}
```

With this program, the output is as follows:

An example of fused multiply-add operation is 10
The larger of two floating point values is 3
The minimum larger of two floating point values is 2
The minimum difference of two floating point values is 0
Absolute value 12

6.1.2 Exponential functions

The below table gives the exponential functions which are available for numbers.

Table 13: Exponential functions

Function	Description
abs	This function is used to compute e raised to a given power
exp2	This function used to compute 2 raised to a given power
log	This function used to compute natural logarithm to base e

Function	Description
log10	This function used to compute common (base 10) logarithm
log2	This function used to compute base 2 logarithm of the given number

Example 27: *The following program is used to showcase the way we can use exponential functions.*

```
#include <iostream>
#include <cstdlib>
#include <cmath>

int main() {

   int d=4;

   std::cout << "e raised to the given power is  " << exp(d) << std::endl;

   std::cout << "2 raised to the given power is  " << exp2(d) << std::endl;

   std::cout << "natural logarithm to base e is " << log(d) << std::endl;

   std::cout << "common (base 10) logarithm is " << log10(d) << std::endl;

   std::cout << "base 2 logarithm of the given number is " << log2(d) << std::endl;
```

```
    return 0;
}
```

With this program, the output is as follows:

e raised to the given power is 54.5982

2 raised to the given power is 16

natural logarithm to base e is 1.38629

common (base 10) logarithm is 0.60206

base 2 logarithm of the given number is 2

6.1.3 Power functions

The below table gives the power functions which are available for numbers.

Table 14: Power functions

Function	Description
sqrt	This function is used to compute the square root of a number
pow	This function is used to compute the raising of a number to the given power
cbrt	This function is used to compute the cubic root of a number
hypot	This function is used to compute the square root of the sum of the squares of two given numbers

Example 28: The following program is used to showcase the way we can use power functions.

```cpp
#include <iostream>
#include <cstdlib>
#include <cmath>

int main() {

    int a=16;
    int b=3;
    int c=27;


    std::cout << "An example of a square root function is  " << sqrt(a) << std::endl;

    std::cout << "An example of the power function is  " << pow(a,b) << std::endl;

    std::cout << "The minimum larger of two floating point values is " << cbrt(c) << std::endl;

    std::cout << "The minimum difference of two floating point values is " << hypot(a,b) << std::endl;


    return 0;

}
```

With this program, the output is as follows:

An example of a square root function is 4
An example of the power function is 4096
The minimum larger of two floating point values is 3
The minimum difference of two floating point values is 16.2788

6.1.4 Trigonometric functions

The below table gives the trigonometric functions which are available for numbers.

Table 15: Trigonometric functions

Function	Description
sin	This function is used to compute the sine equivalent of a given number
cos	This function is used to compute the cosine equivalent of a given number
tan	This function is used to compute the tangent equivalent of a given number
asin	This function is used to compute the arcsine equivalent of a given number
acos	This function is used to compute the arccosine equivalent of a given number
atan	This function is used to compute the arctangent equivalent of a given number

Example 29: ***The following program is used to showcase the way we can use trigonometric functions.***

```
#include <iostream>
#include <cstdlib>
#include <cmath>

int main() {

    int a=45;

    float b=0.34;

    std::cout << "An example of the sine function is " << sin(a) << std::endl;

    std::cout << "An example of the cosine function is " << cos(a) << std::endl;

    std::cout << "An example of the tangent function is " << tan(a) << std::endl;

    std::cout << "An example of the arsine function is " << asin(b) << std::endl;

    std::cout << "An example of the arccosine function is " << acos(b) << std::endl;

    std::cout << "An example of the arctangent function is " << atan(b) << std::endl;

    return 0;

}
```

With this program, the output is as follows:

An example of the sine function is 0.850904

An example of the cosine function is 0.525322

An example of the tangent function is 1.61978

An example of the arsine function is 0.346917

An example of the arccosine function is 1.22388

An example of the arctangent function is 0.327739

6.1.5 Nearest integer floating point functions

The below table gives the nearest integer floating point functions which are available for numbers.

Table 16: Nearest integer floating point functions

Function	Description
ceil	This function gives the nearest integer not less than the given value
floor	This function gives the nearest integer not greater than the given value
trunc	This function gives the nearest integer not greater in magnitude than the given value
round	This function gives the nearest integer, rounding away from zero in halfway cases

Example 30: *The following program is used to showcase the way we can use the above mentioned functions.*

```cpp
#include <iostream>
#include <cstdlib>
#include <cmath>

int main() {

    float a=45.55;

    std::cout << "An example of the ceil function is  " << ceil(a) << std::endl;

    std::cout << "An example of the floor function is  " << floor(a) << std::endl;

    std::cout << "An example of the trunc function is  " << trunc(a) << std::endl;

    std::cout << "An example of the round function is  " << round(a) << std::endl;

    return 0;

}
```

With this program, the output is as follows:

An example of the ceil function is 46

An example of the floor function is 45

An example of the trunc function is 45

An example of the round function is 46

6.1.6 Classification and comparison functions

The below table gives the classification and comparison functions which are available for numbers.

Table 17: Classification and comparison functions

Function	Description
ceil	This function gives the nearest integer not less than the given value

Example 31: The following program is used to showcase the way we can use the above mentioned functions.

```
#include <iostream>
#include <cstdlib>
#include <cmath>

int main() {

    float a=45.55;

    float b=46.66;


    std::cout << "An example of the ceil function is " << std::isfinite(a) << std::endl;

    std::cout << "An example of the floor function is " << std::isinf(a) << std::endl;

    std::cout << "An example of the trunc function is " <<
```

```
    std::isnormal(a) << std::endl;

    std::cout << "An example of the round function is  " <<
std::signbit(a) << std::endl;

    std::cout << "An example of the round function is  " <<
std::isgreater(a,b) << std::endl;

    std::cout << "An example of the round function is  " <<
std::isgreaterequal(a,b) << std::endl;

    std::cout << "An example of the round function is  " <<
std::isless(a,b) << std::endl;

    std::cout << "An example of the round function is  " <<
std::islessequal(a,b) << std::endl;

    std::cout << "An example of the round function is  " <<
std::islessgreater(a,b) << std::endl;

    return 0;

}
```

With this program, the output is as follows:

An example of the ceil function is 1
An example of the floor function is 0
An example of the trunc function is 1
An example of the round function is 0
An example of the round function is 0
An example of the round function is 0
An example of the round function is 1
An example of the round function is 1
An example of the round function is 1

7. Strings

A string is nothing but a sequence of characters which is terminated by the null character to denote that the string has indeed been terminated.

{'H','e','l','l','o','\0'}

The above example shows how the string "Hello" is defined as a sequence of characters with the '/0' as the null character. The below example shows how to define the "World" string in C++.

Example 32: The following program is used to showcase the way we can use strings in C++.

```
#include <iostream>

using namespace std;

int main () {

    char example[6] = {'W', 'o', 'r', 'l', 'd', '\0'};

    cout << example << endl;
    return 0;
}
```

With this program, the output is as follows:

World

Also you don't need to define the dimensions for the array as shown below.

```
#include <iostream>

using namespace std;

int main () {
   char example[] = {'W', 'o', 'r', 'l', 'd', '\0'};

   cout << example << endl;

   return 0;
}
```

You will still get the same output of 'World'. Now let's look at the different functions which are available in C++ for strings.

7.1 Capacity operations

The below section gives the details of the capacity operations available for strings.

Table 18: Capacity operations

Function	Description
size	This function returns the size of the string
length	This function returns the length of the string

Function	Description
max_size	This function returns the maximum size of the string
capacity	This function returns the capacity of the string
clear	This function clears the string
empty	This function checks to see if the string is empty. If yes , then a value of 1 is returned else a value of 0 is returned

Example 33: The following program is used to showcase the capacity functions available on strings.

```
#include <iostream>
#include <string>

using namespace std;

int main () {

    string str="World";

    cout << " The size of the string is " << str.size() << endl;

    cout << " The length of the string is " << str.length() << endl;

    cout << " The maximum size of the string is " << str.max_size() << endl;

    cout << " The capacity of the string is " << str.capacity() << endl;

    str.clear(); // This clears the string
```

```
    cout << " The string is " << str << endl;

    cout << " Is the string empty " << str.empty() << endl;

    return 0;
}
```

With this program, the output is as follows:

The size of the string is 5
The length of the string is 5
The maximum size of the string is 2147483647
The capacity of the string is 15
The length of the string is
The length of the string is 1

7.2 String operations

The below section gives the details of the string operations available for strings.

Table 19: String operations

Function	Description
data	This function returns the data contained in the string
copy	This function is used to copy the contents from one string to the other

Function	Description
find	This function is used to find the presence of one string inside of another
substr	This is used to generate a sub string from the original string
compare	This function is used to compare 2 strings
find_first_of	This function is used to find the presence of a substring in a string
find_last_of	This function is used to find the presence of a substring in a string from the end

Now let's look at each function individually on how they work.

7.2.1 Data function

This function is used to copy the contents from one string to the other.

Example 34: The following program is used to showcase the string data functions.

```
#include <iostream>
#include <string>

using namespace std;

int main () {

   string str="World";
```

```
    // showcasing the data function

    cout << " The data in the string is " << str.data() << endl;


    return 0;
}
```

With this program, the output is as follows:

The data in the string is World

7.2.2 Copy function

The copy function has the following syntax:

```
copy(start,end)
```

Where the start is the starting position from the original string from where the copy should start, and end is the ending position where the copy should end. This function returns the length of string which is copied.

Example 35: The following program is used to showcase the string copy functions.

```
#include <iostream>
#include <string>

using namespace std;

int main () {

    string str="World";
```

```
    char strnew[20];

    int len;

    // showcasing the copy operator
    /* We are first using the copy operator to copy the characters
from position 2
       to position 3 from the original string*/

    len=str.copy(strnew,2,3);

    /* We then get the length of the string which is copied. We then
append the
       null character to the end of the string*/

    strnew[len]='\0';

    cout<<" The new string is " << strnew <<endl;



    return 0;
}
```

With this program, the output is as follows:

The new string is ld

7.2.3 Find function

The find function is used to find the presence of one string inside another. The find function has different variations. So let's look at each variation in detail.

Scenario 1

find(substr)

Where substr is the string which needs to be found.

Example 36: The following program is used to showcase the first variation of the find function.

```
#include <iostream>
#include <string>

using namespace std;

int main () {

    string str="World";

    cout<<"The position of or in the original string is "<<str.find("or")<<endl;

    return 0;
}
```

With this program, the output is as follows:

The position of or in the original string is 1

Scenario 2

find(substr,start,no)

Where substr is the string which needs to be found, start is the starting position in the original string to start from, and no is the number of characters of the search string to consider.

Example 37: The following program is used to showcase the second variation of the find function.

```
#include <iostream>
#include <string>

using namespace std;

int main () {

    string str="This is a whole new World";

    cout<<"The position of is in the original string is "<<
str.find("is",3,2)<<endl;


    return 0;
}
```

With this program, the output is as follows:

The position of is in the original string is 5

7.2.4 Substr function

This function is used to generate the sub string from the original string. The format of the function is:

```
substr(start,no)
```

Where start is the starting position of the substring, and no is the number of characters to consider.

Example 38: *The following program is used to showcase the string substr functions.*

```
#include <iostream>
#include <string>

using namespace std;

int main () {

    string str="This is a whole new World";

    cout<<"An example of the sub string is "<<str.substr(3,8)<<endl;


    return 0;
}
```

With this program, the output is as follows:

An example of the sub string is s is a w

7.2.5 Compare function

The compare function is used to compare two strings. The find function has different variations. So let's look at each variation in detail.

Scenario 1

```
compare(str1)
```

Where str1 is the string which needs to be compared against.

The return values of this function are:

- 0 – This indicates that the strings being compared are equal.

- <0– This indicates that either the value of the first character that does not match is lower in the compared string, or all compared characters match but the compared string is shorter.

- >0– This indicates that either the value of the first character that does not match is greater in the compared string, or all compared characters match but the compared string is longer.

Example 39: The following program is used to showcase the first variation of the compare function.

```
#include <iostream>
#include <string>

using namespace std;

int main () {

    string str="World";

    cout<<"An example of the sub string is "<<
str.compare("World")<<endl;


    return 0;
}
```

With this program, the output is as follows:
An example of the sub string is 0

Scenario 2

compare(start,no,str1)

Where str1 is the string which needs to be compared against, start is the staring position to consider, and no is the number of characters to consider for the search string.

Example 40: The following program is used to showcase the second variation of the compare function.

```
#include <iostream>
#include <string>

using namespace std;

int main () {

    string str="World";

    cout<<"An example of the compare function is "<<
    str.compare(2,3,"or")<<endl;


    return 0;
}
```

With this program, the output is as follows:

An example of the compare function is 1

7.2.6 Find_first_of function

The compare function is used to find the first occurrence of a substring in an original string.

Example 41: The following program is used to showcase the find_first_of.

```
#include <iostream>
#include <string>

using namespace std;

int main () {

    string str="World";

    cout<<"An example of the find first of funtion is "<<
str.find_first_of("o")<<endl;


    return 0;
}
```

With this program, the output is as follows:

An example of the find first of function is 1

7.2.7 find_last_of function

The compare function is used to find the first occurrence of a substring in an original string from the end.

Example 42: The following program is used to showcase the find_last_of.

```
#include <iostream>
#include <string>

using namespace std;

int main () {

   string str="Worlod";

   cout<<"An example of the find last of function is "<<
str.find_last_of("o")<<endl;


   return 0;
}
```

With this program, the output is as follows:

An example of the find last of function is 4

7.3 Modifier functions

The modifier functions can be used to modify the contents of a string. The various modifier functions are given below.

Table 20: String modifier operations

Function	Description
append	This function is used to append a substring to the original string

Function	Description
insert	This function is used to insert a substring to the original string
replace	This function is used to replace a substring inside the original string
pop_back	This function is used to pop one character out of the string
push_back	This function is used to push one character to the string
shrink_to_fit	This function is used to shrink the string to fit the number of characters assigned to the string

Let's now look at each function in more detail.

7.3.1 Append function

The append function is used to append a string to another string. The append function has different variations. So let's look at each variation in detail.

Scenario 1

```
append(str)
```

Where str is the string which needs to be appended to the source string.

Example 43: The following program is used to showcase the first variation of the append function.

```
#include <iostream>
#include <string>

using namespace std;

int main () {
   string str="Hello";

   cout<<"An example of the append function is "<< str.append(" World")<<endl;


   return 0;
}
```

With this program, the output is as follows:

An example of the append function is Hello World

Scenario 2

```
append(str,start,no)
```

Where str is the string which needs to be appended to the source string. Start is the starting position to consider in the append string, and no is the number of characters to append in the source string.

Example 44: The following program is used to showcase the second variation of the append function.

```
#include <iostream>
#include <string>

using namespace std;

int main () {

   string str="Hello";

   cout<<"An example of the append function is "<< str.append(" new World",4,6)<<endl;


   return 0;
}
```

With this program, the output is as follows:

An example of the append function is Hello World

7.3.2 Insert function

The insert function is used to insert a string into another string. The insert function has different variations. So let's look at each variation in detail.

Scenario 1

```
insert(pos,str)
```

Where str is the string which needs to be inserted to the source string, and pos is the position where the string needs to be inserted.

Example 45: The following program is used to showcase the first variation of the insert function.

```
#include <iostream>
#include <string>

using namespace std;

int main () {
    string str="Hello";

    cout<<"An example of the insert function is "<< str.insert(5," World")<<endl;


    return 0;
}
```

With this program, the output is as follows:

An example of the insert function is Hello World

Scenario 2

insert(pos,str,start,no)

Where str is the string which needs to be inserted to the source string, and pos is the position where the string needs to be inserted. Start is the staring position, and no is the number of characters from the new string which needs to be inserted.

Example 46: The following program is used to showcase the second variation of the insert function.

```cpp
#include <iostream>
#include <string>

using namespace std;

int main () {

    string str="Hello";

    cout<<"An example of the append function is "<<
str.insert(5,"new World",3,6)<<endl;

    return 0;
}
```

With this program, the output is as follows:

An example of the insert function is Hello World

7.3.3 Replace function

The replace function is used to replace a string with another string. The replace function has different variations. So let's look at each variation in detail.

Scenario 1

```
replace(str,start,end)
```

Where str is the string which needs to be replaced to the source string. The start and end is the starting and end positions in the source string which need to be replaced.

Example 47: *The following program is used to showcase the first variation of the replace function.*

```
#include <iostream>
#include <string>

using namespace std;

int main () {
   string str="Hello every";

   cout<<"An example of the replace function is "<<
str.replace(6,6,"World")<<endl;


   return 0;
}
```

With this program, the output is as follows:

An example of the replace function is Hello World

Scenario 2

replace(str,start,end,newstart,pos)

Where str is the string which needs to be replaced to the source string. The start and end is the starting and end positions in the source string which need to be replaced.

Newstart is the staring position, and no is the number of characters from the replacing string which needs to be considered.

Example 48: The following program is used to showcase the second variation of the replace function.

```
#include <iostream>
#include <string>

using namespace std;

int main () {

    string str="Hello every";

    cout<<"An example of the replace function is "<<
str.replace(6,6,"new World",4,6)<<endl;


    return 0;
}
```

With this program, the output is as follows:

An example of the replace function is Hello World

7.3.4 Pop_back function

This function is used to pop one character from the string.

Example 49: The following program is used to showcase the pop_back function.

```
#include <iostream>
#include <string>

using namespace std;

int main () {

   string str="World";

   str.pop_back();

   cout<<" The new string is "<<str;


   return 0;
}
```

With this program, the output is as follows:

The new string is Worl

7.3.5 Push_back function

This function is used to push one character to the string.

Example 50: The following program is used to showcase the push_back function.

```
#include <iostream>
#include <string>

using namespace std;
```

```
int main () {

    string str="World";

    str.push_back('a');

    cout<<" The new string is "<<str;


    return 0;
}
```

With this program, the output is as follows:

The new string is Worlda

7.3.6 Shrink_to_fit function

This function is used to shrink the string to fit the number of characters assigned to the string.

Example 51: The following program is used to showcase the shrink to fit function.

```
#include <iostream>
#include <string>

using namespace std;

int main () {

    string str="World";
```

```
    str.resize(3);

    str.shrink_to_fit();

    cout<<" The new string is "<<str;


    return 0;
}
```

With this program, the output is as follows:

The new string is Wor

8. Functions

A function is used to encapsulate code into multiple logical units. Rather than defining all application code inside just the main function, it becomes ideal to split the code into multiple functions. This also helps to maintain the code and ideal when further changes need to be made to the code.

The general definition of a function is given below:

```
return_type functionname( parameter list ) {
  body
}
```

- The return type is the data type which is returned from the function. So functions can be used to return values to the main program.

- The functionname is the name given to the function.

- The parameter list is the list of parameters that can be sent to the function.

- The body contains the main code of the function.

One can then call the function via the function name and pass in any parameters if required. Let's look at different examples of how to use functions.

Example 52: The following program is used to showcase how to use a simple function.

```cpp
#include <iostream>
#include <string>

using namespace std;

void add()
{
   int a=5;

   int b=6;

   cout<<" This function adds 2 numbers "<<a+b;
}

int main () {

add();
   return 0;
}
```

So in the above program we have:

- A function with the name of add.
- The function does not return anything so it has the void return type.
- The function does not take in any parameters for now.
- We then call the add function in the main function.

With this program, the output is as follows:

This function adds 2 numbers 11

Example 53: The following program is used to showcase how to use a simple function with the use of parameters.

```cpp
#include <iostream>
#include <string>

using namespace std;

void add(int a,int b)
{
    cout<<" This function adds 2 numbers "<<a+b;

}

int main () {

add(5,6);

    return 0;
}
```

Now with the above program we are:

- Defining 2 parameters, a and b for the add function.
- We then input the parameters when we call the add function from the main program.

With this program, the output is as follows:

This function adds 2 numbers 11

Example 54: *The following program is used to showcase how to use a simple function with the use of parameters and a return type.*

```
#include <iostream>
#include <string>

using namespace std;

int add(int a,int b)
{
   return a+b;

}

int main () {

   cout<<" This function adds 2 numbers "<<add(5,6);


   return 0;
}
```

Now with the above program we are:

- Defining a return type of integer for the add function.
- We then use the return keyword to return the value to the main program.

With this program, the output is as follows:

This function adds 2 numbers 11

8.1 Default parameters

When using parameters with functions, one can also have a default value assigned to the parameters. Let's look at an example of how we can use default parameters.

Example 55: The following program is used to showcase how to use default parameters.

```
#include <iostream>
#include <string>

using namespace std;

int add(int a,int b=10)
{
   return a+b;

}

int main () {

   cout<<" This function adds 2 numbers "<<add(5);

   return 0;
}
```

Now with the above program we are:

- Defining that parameter b takes in a default value of 10.

With this program, the output is as follows:

This function adds 2 numbers 15

Note that we can also override the default parameter set, by passing a custom value to the parameter.

Example 56: The following program is used to showcase how to override default parameters.

```cpp
#include <iostream>
#include <string>

using namespace std;

int add(int a,int b=10)
{
    return a+b;

}

int main () {

    cout<<" This function adds 2 numbers "<<add(5,12);


    return 0;
}
```

With this program, the output is as follows:

This function adds 2 numbers 17

9. Classes and Objects

A class is used to represent entities. For example, suppose we wanted to represent an employee using C++, we can do this with the help of a class. So the student has be the form of a class and can have something known as properties. These properties can be StudentID , StudentName or anything else that can be used to define the Student. The class can also have methods which can be used to manipulate the properties of the student. So there can be a method which can be used to define the values of the properties and another to display the properties of the student.

The syntax for the definition of a class is:

```
Class classname
{
Class modifier:
Data type Class members;
Data type Class functions;
}
```

Where:

- Classname is the name given to the class.

- The class modifier is the visibility given to either the member or function of a class which can be either private, public or protected.

- We then define the various data members of a class, each of which can have a data type.

- We then have the functions of the class, each of which can accept parameters and also return values of different data types.

So let's look at a quick definition of a class:

```
class Student
{
int studentID;
string studentName;
}
```

So in the above code we have:

- A class with the name of Student.

- Two properties, one is a studentID which has the type integer and studentName which has the type string.

Now in order to define a student with values, we need to define an object of the class. To define an object, we just need to ensure we define the type as that of the class.

```
Student student1;
```

So in the above code, the student1 is the variable of the type Student. We have now defined values to the properties. Now let's look at an example code of how to define classes and objects.

Example 57: The following program is used to showcase how to use classes and objects.

```cpp
#include <iostream>
using namespace std;

// Defining the student class
class Student
{
public:
// The members of the class
   int studentID;

   string studentName;
};

int main () {

// variable of the type student
Student stud1;

   stud1.studentID=1;

   stud1.studentName="John";

cout<<"Student ID "<<stud1.studentID<<endl;

cout<<"Student Name "<<stud1.studentName;

   return 0;
}
```

Now with the above program:

- We have defined a class called Student outside of the main program.

- The Student class has 2 properties. They have the public modifier, we will look at modifier's shortly.

- We then defined an object called stud1 of the type Student.

- We then assign a value of 1 to studentID and John to studentName.

- We then display the values to the console.

With this program, the output is as follows:

Student ID 1

Student Name John

9.1 Member functions

Member functions can be used to add more functionality to the class. The member functions can be used, for example, to output the values of the properties. So you dot need to add code every time to display the values, you can just invoke the function.

So now let's look at an example of how we can use member functions.

Example 58: The following program is used to showcase how to use member functions.

```
#include <iostream>
using namespace std;

class Student
{
```

```
public:
  int studentID;

  string studentName;

  void Display()
  {
    cout<<"Student ID "<<studentID<<endl;

    cout<<"Student Name "<<studentName;

  }
};

int main () {

Student stud1;

  stud1.studentID=1;

  stud1.studentName="John";

  stud1.Display();

  return 0;
}
```

Now with the above program:

- We are now defining a member function called Display() which outputs the studentId and studentName to the console.

- We can then call the member function from the object in the main program.

With this program, the output is as follows:

Student ID 1

Student Name John

Now let's look at a way we can use member functions to take values from the main program.

Example 59: The following program is used to showcase how to use member functions in another way.

```
#include <iostream>
using namespace std;

class Student
{
public:
   int studentID;

   string studentName;

   void Display()
   {
      cout<<"Student ID "<<studentID<<endl;

      cout<<"Student Name "<<studentName;

}
   void Input(int id,string name) {

      studentID=id;

      studentName=name;
   }

};
```

```
int main () {

Student stud1;

   stud1.Input(1,"John");
   stud1.Display();

   return 0;
}
```

Now with the above program:

- We are now defining a member function called Input() which takes in 2 values and assigns it to the studentid and studentName property.

With this program, the output is as follows:

Student ID 1

Student Name John

9.2 Class modifiers

Class modifiers can be used to define the visibility of properties and methods in the class. Below are the various modifiers available.

- Private – With private the properties and methods are only available to the class itself.

- Protected - With protected the properties and methods are only available to the class itself and subclasses derived from the class itself.

- Public - With public the properties and methods are available to all classes.

Let's start with the protected access modifier in the topic for derived classes. So let's look at an example for private modifiers.

Example 60: The following program is used to showcase how to use private access modifiers with an error condition.

```cpp
#include <iostream>
using namespace std;

class Student
{
private:
   int studentID;

   string studentName;

   void Display()
   {
      cout<<"Student ID "<<studentID<<endl;

      cout<<"Student Name "<<studentName;

   }
   void Input(int id,string name) {

      studentID=id;

      studentName=name;
```

```
    }
};

int main () {

Student stud1;

    stud1.Input(1,"John");
    stud1.Display();

    return 0;
}
```

With this program, the output is as follows:

In function 'int main()':

error: 'void Student::Input(int, std::__cxx11::string)' is private

   void Input(int id,string name) {

      ^

error: within this context

   stud1.Input(1,"John");

      ^

'void Student::Display()' is private

   void Display()

Since the access modifier is private, it can only be accessed by the class itself, hence you will get all these errors. The way to resolve this is to define the program as follows.

Example 61: The following program is used to showcase how to use private access modifiers.

```cpp
#include <iostream>
using namespace std;

class Student
{
private:
   int studentID;

   string studentName;
public:
   void Display()
   {
     cout<<"Student ID "<<studentID<<endl;

     cout<<"Student Name "<<studentName;

   }
   void Input(int id,string name) {
     studentID=id;

     studentName=name;

   }
};

int main () {

Student stud1;

   stud1.Input(1,"John");
```

```
    stud1.Display();

    return 0;
}
```

Now with the above program:

- We are defining the properties as private and the methods as public. This is the normal practice for classes.

With this program, the output is as follows:

Student ID 1

Student Name John

One can also define multiple classes in a program and make use of those classes. Let's look at an example of this.

Example 62: The following program is used to showcase how to use multiple classes.

```
#include <iostream>
using namespace std;

class Student
{
private:
   int studentID;

   string studentName;

public:
   void Display()
   {
     cout<<"Student ID "<<studentID<<endl;
```

```cpp
        cout<<"Student Name "<<studentName<<endl;
    }
    void Input(int id,string name) {
        studentID=id;
        studentName=name;
    }
};
class Employee
{
private:
    int employeeID;
    string employeeName;
public:
    void Display()
    {
        cout<<"Employee ID "<<employeeID<<endl;
        cout<<"Employee Name "<<employeeName<<endl;
    }
    void Input(int id,string name) {
        employeeID=id;
        employeeName=name;
    }
};
```

```
int main () {
Student stud1;
    stud1.Input(1,"John");
    stud1.Display();
Employee emp1;
    emp1.Input(2,"Mary");
    emp1.Display();
    return 0;
}
```

Now with the above program:

- We are defining two classes, one is Employee and the other is Student. And we can use both of these classes in the main program.

With this program, the output is as follows:

Student ID 1
Student Name John
Employee ID 2
Employee Name Mary

We can also define multiple objects of a class. Let's look at an example of this.

Example 63: The following program is used to showcase how to define multiple objects.

```cpp
#include <iostream>
using namespace std;

class Student
{
private:
   int studentID;

   string studentName;
public:
   void Display()
   {
      cout<<"Student ID "<<studentID<<endl;

      cout<<"Student Name "<<studentName<<endl;

   }
   void Input(int id,string name) {

      studentID=id;

      studentName=name;
   }

};

int main () {

Student stud1,stud2;

   stud1.Input(1,"John");

   stud1.Display();
```

```
    stud2.Input(2,"Mary");

    stud2.Display();

    return 0;
}
```

With this program, the output is as follows:

Student ID 1
Student Name John
Student ID 2
Student Name Mary

9.3 Constructors

Constructors are special methods in the class which are called when an object of the class is created. The constructor has the name of class. The syntax of the constructor method is shown below:

```
classname()
{
// Define any code for the constructor
}
```

Let's look at an example of how we can use constructors.

Example 64: The following program is used to showcase how to define constructors.

```cpp
#include <iostream>
using namespace std;

class Student
{

private:
   int studentID;

   string studentName;
public:
   Student()
   {
      cout<<"The constructor is being called "<<endl;

      studentID=1;

      studentName="Default";
   }
   void Display()
   {
      cout<<"Student ID "<<studentID<<endl;

      cout<<"Student Name "<<studentName<<endl;

   }
   void Input(int id,string name) {
      studentID=id;

      studentName=name;
   }

};
```

```
int main () {

Student stud1;

    stud1.Display();

    return 0;
}
```

With this program, the output is as follows:

The constructor is being called
Student ID 1
Student Name Default

As you can see from the output, we can see that the constructor gets called when the object is created and assigns the default values to the properties of the class.

We can also change the values of the properties after the constructor is executed. Let's look at an example where we can change the values of the properties after the constructor is called.

Example 65: The following program is used to showcase how to work with properties along with constructors.

```
#include <iostream>
using namespace std;

class Student
{
```

```cpp
private:
    int studentID;

    string studentName;
public:
    Student()
    {
        cout<<"The constructor is being called "<<endl;

        studentID=1;

        studentName="Default";
    }
    void Display()
    {
        cout<<"Student ID "<<studentID<<endl;

        cout<<"Student Name "<<studentName<<endl;

    }
    void Input(int id,string name) {

        studentID=id;

        studentName=name;
    }
};

int main () {

Student stud1;


    stud1.Display();
```

```
    stud1.Input(2,"Joe");

    stud1.Display();

    return 0;
}
```

Now with the above program:

- We are now calling the Input function to change the values of the properties.
- And we are calling the Display function twice to showcase the values of the properties.

With this program, the output is as follows:

The constructor is being called
Student ID 1
Student Name Default
Student ID 2
Student Name Joe

9.4 Parameterized constructors

It is also possible to pass in parameters to the constructor like any other ordinary function. The syntax of the constructor method with parameters is shown below:

```
classname(parameters)
{
// Use the parameters accordingly.
}
```

Let's look at an example on how we can use parameterized constructors.

Example 66: The following program is used to showcase how to work with parameterized constructors.

```cpp
#include <iostream>
using namespace std;

class Student
{

private:
  int studentID;

  string studentName;
public:
  Student(int id,string name)
  {
    cout<<"The constructor is being called "<<endl;

    studentID=id;

    studentName=name;
  }
  void Display()
  {
    cout<<"Student ID "<<studentID<<endl;

    cout<<"Student Name "<<studentName<<endl;

  }
  void Input(int id,string name) {
    studentID=id;

    studentName=name;
```

```
    }
};

int main () {

Student stud1(1,"Joe");

   stud1.Display();

   stud1.Input(2,"Mary");

   stud1.Display();

   return 0;
}
```

Now with the above program:

- We are defining a constructor which takes in parameters. We are then assigning the parameters to the properties in the constructor.

With this program, the output is as follows:

The constructor is being called

Student ID 1

Student Name Joe

Student ID 2

Student Name Mary

9.5 Destructors

Destructors are special methods in the class which are called when an object of the class is destroyed. The constructor has the name of class along with the ~ character. The syntax of the destructor method is shown below:

```
~classname
{
}
```

Let's look at an example of how we can use destructors.

Example 67: The following program is used to showcase how to work with destructors.

```
#include <iostream>
using namespace std;

class Student
{

private:
   int studentID;

   string studentName;
public:
   Student(int id,string name)
   {
     cout<<"The constructor is being called "<<endl;

     studentID=id;

     studentName=name;
   }
   void Display()
   {
```

```cpp
        cout<<"Student ID "<<studentID<<endl;

        cout<<"Student Name "<<studentName<<endl;

    }
    void Input(int id,string name) {
        studentID=id;

        studentName=name;
    }
    ~Student()
    {
        cout<<" The destructor is being called "<<endl;
    }
};

int main () {

Student stud1(1,"Joe");

    stud1.Display();

    return 0;
}
```

Now with the above program:

- We are defining a destructor function which has the class name along with the ~ character.

With this program, the output is as follows:

The constructor is being called

Student ID 1

Student Name Joe

The destructor is being called

From the output you will now see that the destructor is being called before the program exits. When an object is destroyed, the destructor automatically gets called.

9.6 Static members

Static members are used to define values that should remain the same across all objects of a class. Since classes have properties which are separate for each object, sometimes there is a requirement for having properties that never change. This can be done with static members. The syntax of a static member is defined below:

```
Class classname
{
static datatype staticmembername
}
```

Here the static keyword is used to showcase that a static member is being defined. If you want to initialize the static data member, this can be done outside of the class as follows:

```
datatype classname::staticmembername = value;
```

Let's look at an example of how we can achieve this.

Example 68: The following program is used to showcase how to work with static members.

```cpp
#include <iostream>
using namespace std;

class Student
{

private:
  int studentID;

  string studentName;

public:
  static int counter;

  Student()
  {
    cout<<"The constructor is being called "<<endl;

    counter++;
  }
  void DisplayCounter()
  {

    cout<<"The value of the counter is "<<counter<<endl;

  }
  void Display()
  {
    cout<<"Student ID "<<studentID<<endl;

    cout<<"Student Name "<<studentName<<endl;

  }
```

```cpp
    void Input(int id,string name) {
        studentID=id;
        studentName=name;
    }
};

int Student::counter=0;

int main () {

Student stud1;

stud1.DisplayCounter();

Student stud2;

stud2.DisplayCounter();

    return 0;
}
```

With this program, the output is as follows:

The constructor is being called
The value of the counter is 1
The constructor is being called
The value of the counter is 2

10. Arrays

Arrays are used to define a collection of values of a similar datatype. The definition of a data type is shown below:

Datatype arrayname[arraysize]

The arraysize is the number of elements that can be defined for the array. Let's now look at an example of how we can define an array in C++.

Example 69: The following program is used to showcase how to work with arrays.

```
#include <iostream>
using namespace std;

int main () {

int collect[3];

   collect[0]=1;

   collect[1]=2;

   collect[2]=3;
```

```
    return 0;
}
```

Now with the above program:

- We are defining an integer array which has a size of 3.

- The first item in the array starts with the 0 index value.

- Each value of the array can be accessed with its corresponding index value. Each value of the array is also known as the element of the array.

Let's now look at an example of how we can display the values of the array.

Example 70: The following program is used to showcase how to work with arrays and display the elements of the array.

```
#include <iostream>
using namespace std;

int main () {

    int collect[3];
    collect[0]=1;

    collect[1]=2;

    collect[2]=3;

    cout<<" The first element of the array is "<<collect[0]<<endl;

    cout<<" The second element of the array is "<<collect[1]<<endl;
```

```
    cout<<" The third element of the array is "<<collect[2]<<endl;

    return 0;
}
```

With this program, the output is as follows:

The first element of the array is 1

The second element of the array is 2

The third element of the array is 3

We can also define an array of different data types other than the integer data type. Let's look at another example where we can define an array of strings.

Example 71: The following program is used to showcase how to work with string arrays.

```
#include <iostream>
using namespace std;


int main () {

    string collect[3];

    collect[0]="First";

    collect[1]="Second";

    collect[2]="Third";

    cout<<" The first element of the array is "<<collect[0]<<endl;
```

```
    cout<<" The second element of the array is "<<collect[1]<<endl;

    cout<<" The third element of the array is "<<collect[2]<<endl;

    return 0;
}
```

With this program, the output is as follows:

The first element of the array is First
The second element of the array is Second
The third element of the array is Third

We can also carry out the normal operations with the elements of the array as we would normally do with ordinary variables. Let's look at an example on how we can work with the elements of the array.

Example 72: The following program is used to showcase how to work with arrays elements with standard operators.

```
#include <iostream>
using namespace std;

int main () {

    string collect[3];

    collect[0]="First";

    collect[1]="Second";

    collect[2]="Third";
```

```
    int team[3];

    team[0]=1;

    team[1]=2;

    team[2]=3;

    cout<<" The sum of the elements of the integer array is "<<team[0]+team[1]+team[2]<<endl;
    cout<<" The elements of the string array are "<<collect[0]+collect[1]+collect[2]<<endl;

    return 0;
}
```

With this program, the output is as follows:

The sum of the elements of the integer array is 6

The elements of the string array are

FirstSecondThird

10.1 Initializing arrays

Arrays can also be initialized when they are defined. The syntax for the array definition is given below:

Datatype arrayname[N]={value1,value2...valueN-1}

Where the values for the array are defined in the parenthesis { }. Let's now look at an example of this.

Example 73: The following program is used to showcase how to initialize arrays.

```cpp
#include <iostream>
using namespace std;


int main () {

   string collect[3]={"First","Second","Third"};

   int team[3]={1,2,3};

   cout<<" The sum of the elements of the integer array is "<<team[0]+team[1]+team[2]<<endl;
   cout<<" The elements of the string array are "<<collect[0]+collect[1]+collect[2]<<endl;

   return 0;
}
```

With this program, the output is as follows:

The sum of the elements of the integer array is 6

The elements of the string array are

FirstSecondThird

10.2 Going through the elements of the array

When an array has a number of elements, we might need to use the loops available in C++ to iterate through the elements of the array. Let's look at an example of how we can use the loops to iterate through the elements of an array.

Example 74: The following program is used to showcase how to iterate through the elements of the array.

```
#include <iostream>
using namespace std;


int main () {

  int team[10];

  for(int i=0;i<=10;i++)

  {

    team[i]=i;

  }
  // Printing the values of the elements of the array

  for(int i=0;i<=10;i++)
  {

    cout<<"The value of team["<<i<<"] is "<<team[i]<<endl;


  }
    return 0;
}
```

With this program, the output is as follows:

The value of team[0] is 0

The value of team[1] is 1

The value of team[2] is 2
The value of team[3] is 3
The value of team[4] is 4
The value of team[5] is 5
The value of team[6] is 6
The value of team[7] is 7
The value of team[8] is 8
The value of team[9] is 9
The value of team[10] is 10

10.3 Multidimensional arrays

One can also define multidimensional arrays which have different dimensions. The most common form of a multidimensional array is the 2 dimensional array. The below table shows how the array is structured if the following array is defined:

| Collect[3][2] |

Where 3 is the number of rows and 2 is the number of columns. So the array can have a maximum of 6 values.

	Column 0	Column 1
Row 0	1	2
Row 1	3	4
Row 2	5	6

Example 75: *The following program is used to showcase how to define a two dimensional array.*

```
#include <iostream>
using namespace std;

int main () {

  int collect[3][2];

  collect[0][0]=1;

  collect[0][1]=2;

  collect[1][0]=3;

  collect[1][1]=4;

  collect[2][0]=5;

  collect[2][1]=6;

  cout<<" Value at collect[0][0] is "<<collect[0][0]<<endl;

  cout<<" Value at collect[0][1] is "<<collect[0][1]<<endl;

  cout<<" Value at collect[1][0] is "<<collect[1][0]<<endl;

  cout<<" Value at collect[1][1] is "<<collect[1][1]<<endl;

  cout<<" Value at collect[2][0] is "<<collect[2][0]<<endl;

  cout<<" Value at collect[2][1] is "<<collect[2][1]<<endl;

}
```

With this program, the output is as follows:

Value at collect[0][0] is 1

Value at collect[0][1] is 2

Value at collect[1][0] is 3

Value at collect[1][1] is 4

Value at collect[2][0] is 5

Value at collect[2][1] is 6

It becomes easier to use loops when iterating through multi-dimensional arrays in the same way we do for normal arrays. Let's see how we can do this. But this time around since we have 2 dimensions we also need to use nested for loops to iterate through all the elements of the array.

Example 76: The following program is used to showcase how to iterate through a two dimensional array.

```
#include <iostream>
using namespace std;

int main () {

    int collect[3][2];

    collect[0][0]=1;

    collect[0][1]=2;

    collect[1][0]=3;
```

```
    collect[1][1]=4;

    collect[2][0]=5;

    collect[2][1]=6;

    for (int i=0;i<3;i++)

    {
       for (int j=0;j<2;j++)

       {

          cout<<" Value at collect["<<i<<"]["<<j<<"] is "<<collect[i][j]<<endl;

       }
    }

}
```

With this program, the output is as follows:

Value at collect[0][0] is 1
Value at collect[0][1] is 2
Value at collect[1][0] is 3
Value at collect[1][1] is 4
Value at collect[2][0] is 5
Value at collect[2][1] is 6

10.4 Arrays as parameters

Arrays can also be passed as parameters to functions and accessed like normal variables. Let's look at an example of how we can achieve this.

Example 77: The following program is used to showcase how to pass arrays as parameters.

```
#include <iostream>
using namespace std;


void Display(int pcollect[])
{

   cout<<pcollect[0];
   cout<<pcollect[1];
   cout<<pcollect[2];
}

int main () {

int collect[3];

   collect[0]=1;
   collect[1]=2;
   collect[2]=3;

   Display(collect);
}
```

With this program, the output is as follows:

123

11. Data Structure

The data structure type is used to combine data items into a logical unit. Each data item can be of a different type. Structures are used to store the records, which was the commonly used way to store data in the past. The syntax of the structure data type is shown below:

```
struct structurename
{
Datatype membername1;
Datatype membername2;
..
Datatype membernameN;
}variable name;
```

Where:

- Structurename is the name of the structure.

- Membername is the name of the various members in the data structure.

- Variable name is the variable assigned to the data structure.

An example of the declaration of a structure in a C++ program is given below:

```
#include <iostream>
using namespace std;

int main () {

struct Student
{
   int studentID;

   string studentName;

}student1;


}
```

11.1 Accessing the members of the structure

The members of the structure can be accessed via the dot operator. Let's look at an example of how this can be achieved.

Example 78: The following program is used to showcase how to access members of a structure.

```
#include <iostream>
using namespace std;

int main () {

struct Student
{
   int studentID;

   string studentName;
```

```
}student1;

   student1.studentID=1;

   student1.studentName="Mark";

   cout<<"The student ID is "<<student1.studentID<<endl;

   cout<<"The student name is "<<student1.studentName<<endl;
}
```

With this program, the output is as follows:

The student ID is 1

The student name is Mark

One can also define multiple variables of the structure. Let's look at an example of this.

Example 79: The following program is used to showcase how to define multiple variables of a data structure.

```
#include <iostream>
using namespace std;

int main () {

struct Student
{
   int studentID;

   string studentName;
```

```
}student1,student2;
    student1.studentID=1;
    student1.studentName="Mark";
    cout<<"The student 1 ID is "<<student1.studentID<<endl;
    cout<<"The student 1 name is "<<student1.studentName<<endl;
    student2.studentID=2;
    student2.studentName="Joe";
    cout<<"The student 2 ID is "<<student2.studentID<<endl;
    cout<<"The student 2 name is "<<student2.studentName<<endl;
}
```

With this program, the output is as follows:

The student 1 ID is 1
The student 1 name is Mark
The student 2 ID is 2
The student 2 name is Joe

11.2 Passing structures as parameters

The structures can also be passed as parameters to functions. Let's look at an example of how we can pass structures as parameters.

Example 80: The following program is used to showcase how to data structures as parameters.

```cpp
#include <iostream>
using namespace std;

struct Student
{
  int studentID;

  string studentName;

}student1,student2;

void Display(Student pstudent)
{

  cout<<"The student ID is "<<pstudent.studentID<<endl;

  cout<<"The student name is "<<pstudent.studentName<<endl;
}
int main () {

  student1.studentID=1;

  student1.studentName="Mark";

  cout<<"The student 1 ID is "<<student1.studentID<<endl;

  cout<<"The student 1 name is "<<student1.studentName<<endl;

  student2.studentID=2;

  student2.studentName="Joe";
```

```
    cout<<"The student 2 ID is "<<student2.studentID<<endl;

    cout<<"The student 2 name is "<<student2.studentName<<endl;

    Display(student2);

}
```

With this program, the output is as follows:

The student 1 ID is 1

The student 1 name is Mark

The student 2 ID is 2

The student 2 name is Joe

The student ID is 2

The student name is Joe

12. Pointers

Before we move into pointers, we just need to have a quick view on how values of variables are stored in a C++ program. Each value is stored in a memory location. And each memory location has a memory address assigned to it. This is how the program knows where it should go to find the value of a particular variable. The memory location of a variable can be accessed by using the ampersand & operator.

Let's look at an example of how we can access the address of a memory location.

Example 81: The following program is used to showcase how to address memory locations.

```
#include <iostream>
using namespace std;

int main () {

    int i;

    i=10;

    cout<<" The value of i is "<<i<<endl;
```

```
cout<<" The memory address value of i is "<<&i<<endl;
}
```

With this program, the output is as follows:

The value of i is 10

The memory address value of i is 0x61ff1c

One thing that needs to be noted is that the value of the memory address will change depending on what the memory location is that has been assigned by the program at run time.

So now we come to pointers. Pointers are variables which are used to point to a memory location which contains a value. The pointer variable is designated with the * operator. An example of a pointer variable is shown below:

```
int *p;
```

So p is the pointer which points to a memory location which contains an integer value. Similarly if a memory location contains a floating value, then we need to define the pointer as shown below:

```
float *p;
```

Now let's look at a program which defines pointers.

Example 82: The following program is used to showcase how to define pointers.

```
#include <iostream>
using namespace std;


int main () {

  int i;

  i=10;

  cout<<" The value of i is "<<i<<endl;

  cout<<" The memory address value of i is "<<&i<<endl;

  //defining the pointer
  int *p;

  p=&i;

  cout<<" The value of i is "<<*p<<endl;

}
```

From the above program we can:

- See that we are defining a pointer variable p which points to an integer location.

- We then point the pointer to the memory location of the i variable.

- We can then access the value of i via the point p.

With this program, the output is as follows:

The value of i is 10

The memory address value of i is 0x61ff18

The value of i is 10

12.1 Pointer arithmetic

Arithmetic operators can be applied to pointers as well. The best way to look at this is to work with arrays. We can point a pointer to the first value of the array and then increment the pointer to point to the next value in the array.

Let's look at an example on this.

Example 83: The following program is used to showcase how to use pointer arithmetic.

```
#include <iostream>
using namespace std;

int main () {

    int *i;

    int value[3]={1,2,3};

    i=value;

    cout<<" The value is "<<*i<<endl;

    i++;

    cout<<" The value is "<<*i<<endl;
}
```

With this program, the output is as follows:

The value is 1
The value is 2

12.2 Pointers to functions

We can also pass in memory locations to functions which can be used to work with pointers as parameters. Let's look at an example on this.

Example 84: The following program is used to showcase how to use pointers in functions.

```cpp
#include <iostream>
using namespace std;

void Display(int *l)
{
   cout<<"The value is "<<*l;
}

int main () {

   int value=1;

   Display(&value);

}
```

With this program, the output is as follows:

The value is 1

13. Date and Time

In C++ there are data types assigned for date and time. The structure of the date time structure is shown below:

```
struct tm {

  int tm_sec;  // seconds of minutes from 0 to 61

  int tm_min;  // minutes of hour from 0 to 59

  int tm_hour; // hours of day from 0 to 24

  int tm_mday; // day of month from 1 to 31

  int tm_mon;  // month of year from 0 to 11

  int tm_year; // year since 1900

  int tm_wday; // days since Sunday

  int tm_yday; // days since January 1st

  int tm_isdst; // hours of daylight savings time

}
```

Let's now look at an example of how to use date and time in C++.

Example 85: The following program is used to showcase how to use date and time in C++.

```cpp
#include <iostream>
#include <ctime>

using namespace std;

int main( ) {
    // current date/time based on current system
    time_t now = time(0);
    // The date time will be in a raw format which needs to be converted to a string format
    // The ctime is used to convert to a readable string format
    char* dt = ctime(&now);
    cout<<dt;
}
```

With this program, the output is as follows:

Sat Mar 18 01:14:24 2017

Another function available in the date and time library is the clock function, which is like a stopwatch. It can be used to see how long a program has been running. Let's look at an example of how we can use the clock function.

Example 86: The following program is used to showcase how to use the clock function in C++.

```cpp
#include <iostream>
#include <ctime>
#include <unistd.h>
```

```
using namespace std;

int main( ) {

    clock_t start_t, end_t, total_t;
    int i;

    start_t = clock();

for(int i=0;i<10;i++)
{
sleep(10);
}
    end_t = clock();

    total_t = end_t - start_t;
    cout<<total_t;

}
```

The total time spent will differ from system to system. But what happens in the program above is that the clock function starts when the clock function is invoked and is then stopped when the clock function is invoked again.

Conclusion

This has brought us to the end of this book, but it doesn't mean your C++ journey should end here. If you enjoyed this guide, be sure to keep a lookout for the next book in the series that covers more advanced topics of C++.

Lastly, this book was written not only to be a teaching guide, but also a reference manual. So remember to always keep it near, as you venture through this wonderful world of programming

About the Author

Nathan Clark is an expert programmer with nearly 20 years of experience in the software industry.

With a master's degree from MIT, he has worked for some of the leading software companies in the United States and built up extensive knowledge of software design and development.

Nathan and his wife, Sarah, started their own development firm in 2009 to be able to take on more challenging and creative projects. Today they assist high-caliber clients from all over the world.

Nathan enjoys sharing his programming knowledge through his book series, developing innovative software solutions for their clients and watching classic sci-fi movies in his free time.

Made in the USA
Columbia, SC
20 May 2018